UNIVERSITY OF MINNESOTA

Eugene O'Neill

BY JOHN GASSNER

UNIVERSITY OF MINNESOTA PRESS · MINNEAPOLIS

Printed in the United States of America at
the North Central Publishing Company, St. Paul

Library of Congress Catalog Card Number: 65-63409

Distributed to high schools in the United States by Webster Division
McGraw-Hill Book Company
St. Louis   New York   San Francisco   Dallas

PUBLISHED IN GREAT BRITAIN, INDIA, AND PAKISTAN BY THE OXFORD UNIVERSITY
PRESS, LONDON, BOMBAY, AND KARACHI, AND IN CANADA BY THE COPP
CLARK PUBLISHING CO. LIMITED, TORONTO

FOR MAX COSMAN
amicus usque ad aras

JOHN GASSNER is the Sterling Professor of Playwriting and Dramatic Literature at Yale University. He has been a drama critic and contributing editor to numerous publications and is the author or editor of many books on the theater.

Eugene O'Neill

W HEN Eugene O'Neill received the Nobel Prize in 1936 he was in his forty-ninth year and appeared to have concluded his career. More than thirty-five short and long plays by him had been produced in the United States, and they had won him important awards in his own country and an international reputation. But a long period of absence from the theater followed *Days without End*, which had opened in New York on January 8, 1934, and O'Neill did not return with a new play until the Theatre Guild production of *The Iceman Cometh* in 1946. Another decade of absence from the New York stage then ensued when his next play, *A Moon for the Misbegotten*, was withdrawn from a trial tour in the Midwest by O'Neill and the Theatre Guild management. Not until 1956 did another new play by him, *Long Day's Journey into Night*, reach New York. In the meantime, O'Neill had died in Boston on November 27, 1953, so that his renewed career as a dramatist, concluded by this more or less autobiographical drama and three other new pieces (*A Touch of the Poet, More Stately Mansions*, and the one-act play *Hughie*), was mainly posthumous. It may be said that O'Neill, who performed many other feats of endurance in the theater, happened to have two careers in it rather than the customary single one.

O'Neill also attracted attention with two styles of theater rather than one, being equally adept in the styles of realism and expressionism, and with two radically disproportionate types of drama, since he was equally effective in one-act plays and in cyclopean dramas twice the normal length of modern plays. His search for expressive form, in his case a combination of private compul-

5

sions and public ambitions to incorporate modern ideas and notions about life and dramatic art, led him to undertake numerous experiments with symbolic figures, masks, interior monologues, split personalities, choruses, scenic effects, rhythms, and schematizations. In O'Neill's work there is a veritable *summa* of the modern theater's aspirations and achievements as well as its more or less inevitable limitations and failures. It is largely this multifarious engagement with the possibilities of dramatic art, combined with an endeavor to apply them to significant as well as very personally felt subject matter, that made O'Neill a playwright of international importance.

In all his major work O'Neill traced the course of a modern dramatist in search of an aesthetic and spiritual center. It is not certain that he found it often, if ever, but the labor involved in the effort was usually impressive and sometimes notably rewarding. His plays embodied the ideas and conflicts of the first half of the twentieth century, assimilated its advances in dramatic art and theatrical technique, and expressed its uneasy aspirations toward tragic insights and dramatic vision. His impressiveness as a dramatist is ultimately, in fact, the result of his determined effort to trace a thread of meaning in the universe virtually emptied of meaning by a century of scientific and sociological thought. He did not, it is true, find any comforting assurances in the world, but he had the integrity to acknowledge his failure and the persistence to dramatize it with much penetration into human nature. O'Neill's experiments were not undertaken to suit the whims of a volatile trifler or the calculations of a theatrical opportunist bent on following the latest fashion; they manifest, rather, a unity of high purpose rarely exhibited by modern playwrights.

Eugene Gladstone O'Neill was born on October 16, 1888, in a hotel room in the very heart of New York's theatrical district applauded and derided as "Broadway." He was the son of the mat-inee idol and successful actor-manager James O'Neill, who amassed a fortune touring in a melodrama based on Alexandre Dumas' famous romantic novel *The Count of Monte Cristo*. The playwright who took so many successful liberties with dramatic form was entirely at home in the theater, and later also acted in his father's theatrical company. But it early became distressing-ly evident to his parent that the young O'Neill was a rebel who would be more inclined to revolt against the romantic tradition than to preserve it. O'Neill was born into a tragically disturbed family (his mother suffered from drug addiction and his elder brother was a confirmed alcoholic) and had an unstable child-hood, touring the United States with his parents and receiving an irregular education in different private boarding schools. "Usu-ally," O'Neill declared to a reporter in 1932, "a child has a regular, fixed home, but you might say I started as a trouper. I knew only actors and the stage. My mother nursed me in the wings and in dressing rooms." Encouraged by his irresponsible actor-brother James, he was inducted into the bohemian life of the theatrical world at a tender age. After a year at Princeton University, he was suspended in 1907 for a student prank. In 1909 he entered into a secret marriage, later dissolved. That same year he went prospecting for gold in Central America with a mining engineer. Having contracted malaria in the course of this fruitless expedi-tion, he returned to his parents and joined his father's company as an actor and assistant manager for a brief period.

Growing restless again, he shipped to Buenos Aires on a Nor-wegian vessel and found employment for a time with American companies located in the area — an electric company, a packing plant, the Singer Sewing Machine Company. Tiring of clerical employment, he took a job on a cattle boat, tending mules while voyaging from Buenos Aires to South Africa. On his return to

7

Argentina, he found himself unemployed and fell into a state
of destitution which came to a close when he joined a British
vessel bound for New York, but he promptly relapsed into a life
of dissipation on the New York waterfront, frequenting a disreputable tavern, "Jimmy-the-Priest's," which he was to re-create in
the milieu of two of his best known plays, *Anna Christie* and
The Iceman Cometh. Still attracted to the sea, however, he became an able seaman on the American Line and made a voyage
to Southampton, England, before deciding to settle down to a
less adventurous mode of life.

After joining his father's company again and playing a small
part in *Monte Cristo*, followed by several months of intemperate
living, he went to New London in Connecticut, where the family
had its summer home, and joined the staff of the local newspaper, the *New London Telegraph*, as a reporter. He had begun
to publish humorous poetry in a column of that newspaper when
his journalistic career was abruptly terminated by a blow O'Neill
could only consider ironic fate. His health undermined by his
profligate mode of life, he succumbed to tuberculosis and had to
be hospitalized in 1912. A term of six months in a sanatorium,
however, proved to be doubly beneficial: it arrested the disease
and made an avid reader and introspective artist of O'Neill. He
read widely during his convalescence, falling under the influence
of the Greek tragic poets and Strindberg. He began to write plays
in 1913, and in 1914 enrolled in a course in playwriting given at
Harvard University by the famous Professor George Pierce Baker.

The next year he moved to Greenwich Village, then regarded
as the progressive "Left Bank" of New York, and in 1916 joined
an avant-garde group of writers and artists who had established
an amateur theatrical company. Their first season in the summer
of 1915 had been presented on an abandoned wharf in the artists' colony of Provincetown, on Cape Cod, Massachusetts, and

8

they came to call themselves the Provincetown Players. O'Neill began to write short plays for them and soon became their foremost playwright as well as one of their directors when they moved to a small theater in Greenwich Village on Macdougal Street, where theatrical experiments continued to be unfolded long after the dissolution of this company. (The best known of these have been Samuel Beckett's *Krapp's Last Tape* and Edward Albee's *The Zoo Story*.) O'Neill and his associates, the critic Kenneth Macgowan and the great American scenic artist Robert Edmond Jones, also ran a second enterprise, the Greenwich Village Theatre, from 1923 to 1927. In these years at one or the other of the theaters were produced such varied plays as Strindberg's exotic *The Spook Sonata*, O'Neill's own expressionist race-drama *All God's Chillun Got Wings*, and his naturalistic New England variant on the Phaedra-Hippolytus theme, *Desire under the Elms*. Both the Provincetown and the Greenwich Village ventures were among the most influential of groups in the seminal "little theater" movement which gained momentum after 1912 and succeeded in modernizing the American theater in the 1920's by bringing it abreast of European developments in dramatic art and at the same time discovering American backgrounds and rhythms.

The importance of O'Neill's early association with "the Provincetown" can hardly be exaggerated. He found an acceptable channel for his dramatic talent and theatrical interest because he also had an outlet for his personal rebellion in associating himself with an enterprise created by bohemian rebels against materialistic American society and the commercialism of the professional theater. In writing for the Provincetown Players and having his early plays performed before a small public of artists and intellectuals, he escaped the necessity of conforming to the popular taste to which his father had catered all his life with old-fashioned romantic theatricality. The prodigal son could deal with the life he had come to know during his years of wandering, poverty, dissipation, and desperation among common men and fellow-exiles from respectable society. As a result, O'Neill made himself, in his early short plays about the seafaring life (especially those collected under the title of *S. S. Glencairn*), the first American "naturalist" in a period when the general public in America was still expecting from its playwrights discreet pictures of reality that would give no offense. At the same time, his early plays evoked a vigorous poetry of naturalism compounded of the atmosphere of the sea and the moods of the men for whom their life on ships and on the waterfront was both an occupation and an occasion for romantic escape. For O'Neill himself the sea was a symbol of the lostness of mankind in a hostile or indifferent universe, of a conspiracy of Nature against Man. Had he started his career thirty years later — say, in 1945 rather than 1915 — he might indeed have been enrolled in the ranks of Existentialist writers, and another decade later in the company of the "Theater of the Absurd" playwrights.

It would appear that O'Neill became a significant figure in America because his early work was a natural synthesis of both the naturalistic and the poetic strivings of the modern theater. He combined realism of characterization with a sensitive regard for the romantic longings of characters, a naturalist's concern for environmental detail with a metaphysical flight from the particular to the general, and plodding realistic prose with a poetic flair for imagery, atmosphere, and scenic imagination; it could be said of him that he was one of the least poetic and at the same time one of the most poetic of modern dramatists.

This synthesis was apparent virtually from the beginning of his work, in the one-act plays that first drew attention to him. The cultivation of one-act drama was characteristic of the entire avant-garde movement of the period. The Provincetown Players, along with other progressive "little theaters," favored this genre for a variety of reasons. One-act plays required less professional experience to write than full-length dramas, and these novices of the theater found one-act playwriting especially congenial because it enabled them to dispense with the complicated contrivances of plot they despised as unauthentic and artificial. One-act plays were also inexpensive to produce and easy to perform by the amateurs of the little theater movement. (The same tendency to favor the one-act drama had been marked among avant-garde writers for Antoine's Théâtre Libre between 1887 and 1890 and for the Irish national theater, the Abbey in Dublin, before 1914.) With his decisive success in this genre, O'Neill emerged as the foremost product of the little theater in America and its major justification.

O'Neill started with short "slice-of-life" dramas dealing with the miseries, delusions, and obsessions of men adrift in the world. With the appearance of the *S. S. Glencairn* cycle of sea-pieces, beginning with the Provincetown Players' production of his atmospheric drama of the death of a common sailor, *Bound East for Cardiff*, in the summer of 1916, he became the undisputed master of the one-act play form in America. The sharply etched playlets *In the Zone* and *The Long Voyage Home* (1917) and another atmospheric piece, *The Moon of the Caribbees* (1918), along with O'Neill's first Provincetown production, made up the remarkable quartet of one-acters subsequently produced under the collective title of *S. S. Glencairn*. A number of independent pieces such as *Ile* (1917), *The Rope* (1918), and *Where the Cross Is Made* (1918) also enhanced their young author's reputation by the end of World War I. *Ile* is especially representative of his early naturalistic-symbolic style with its mordant treatment of a New England sea captain's obsessive pride in his ability to hunt whales for their "ile" (that is, oil) which drives his lonely wife mad. This little play exemplified O'Neill's taste for tragic irony, his characteristic concern with destructive obsessiveness that resembles the *hybris* of classic tragedy, and his fascination with the sea as a mystery and a seduction, and as a symbol of the malignity of fate.

The same interests soon appeared in a richer and more complicated context when O'Neill began to write his early full-length plays. He gave his sense of tragic irony full scope in the first of these, the saturnine drama of fate and frustration *Beyond the Horizon*, produced in New York in 1920. A country lad who longs to go to sea attracts a farm girl with his dreamy romantic personality and is condemned by an unsuitable marriage to a routine life on the farm for which he is utterly unfit while his practical-minded brother and disappointed rival in love, who was cut out to be a farmer, departs for strange lands and leads a life of adventure for which he has no particular liking. The thwarted romantic man, Robert Mayo, is an absolute failure on the farm and his marriage is destroyed by poverty and domestic recriminations while, ironically, his unromantic brother Andrew actually prospers for a while in his adventuring and amasses a fortune (which he later loses) in romantic surroundings from which the other brother is forever barred. Only death holds the prospect of sailing "beyond the horizon" to the dying Robert Mayo for whom life on the farm had been ensnarement and defeat. Blinded by the sexual instinct, the characters made the wrong choices in life and destroyed their chances of happiness.

In *Anna Christie*, first produced under a different title in 1920 and successfully revived a year later, it is the attraction of the sea that is blamed for the combination of circumstances making a prostitute of the heroine. She had been neglected by her father, a sea captain incapable of resisting the seductions of seafaring life. The captain, unable to understand his own behavior and overwhelmed by his sense of failure as a father, speaks of the sea as a demon and equates it with diabolic fate. And in *Diff'rent*, also produced in 1920, fate plays an ironic trick on a New England girl who broke off her engagement because her seagoing fiancé was not chaste enough to satisfy her puritanical principles; having doomed herself to a life of lonely spinsterhood, she ultimately rebels against frustration by succumbing to a designing rascal many years younger than herself. Whereas *Diff'rent* made crude use of both the irony of fate and the theme of sexual repression attributed by O'Neill's generation to the rigors of New England puritanism, *Anna Christie* moved naturally and smoothly up to its climax, the rejection of Anna by a young Irishman on his discovering her sordid past. Only the ending of the play seemed marred by vaguely promising a reunion between the lovers. (O'Neill himself was apologetic for this concession to sentiment.) But even the concluding scene in which Anna's lover and her father have signed up for a sea voyage after a drinking bout possessed a raffish mordancy that suited the subject and tone of the work, and did not impair the effectiveness of this justifiably popular play. Although O'Neill's dissatisfaction with it arose from a belief that he must write unalloyed tragedies to fulfill his vision of life and his destiny as a significant tragedian, he nevertheless had no reason to be ashamed of what he had accomplished in this play. He had achieved a wry tragicomedy enriched with fully flavored naturalism in dialogue and background that proved satisfying to playgoers in America and abroad, gave the play a good run on Broadway in the theatrical season of 1921–22, and won for its author a second Pulitzer Prize. (He had first received this coveted award the year before with *Beyond the Horizon*.)

In one way or another, the characters in these and other early works were entangled with circumstances which if not tragic in any strict sense of the term were destructive of happiness, and O'Neill was by no means a poor judge of his potentialities as a dramatist in believing that his forte was tragedy. He was least successful when the quality of the characters and their conflicts fell short of tragic dimension or elevation, as was the case in several minor works that followed *Anna Christie*. The earliest of these, *The Straw*, produced in 1921, dealt with the love of two tubercular patients in a sanatorium, one of whom is cured after a few months and leaves behind him the girl, whose situation is hopeless and is alleviated only by the illusion that she will join him some day. In *The First Man* (1922) a scientist, who is deficient in tragic stature, destroys his prospects of happiness by resenting the intrusion of a child into his married life; and in *Welded* (1924), a play clearly written under the influence of Strindberg although also steeped in personal experience, husband and wife are consumed with resentment while drawn to each other so powerfully by an irrational force that they cannot live apart. But it was not long before O'Neill lifted himself out of the morass of petty and pathetic situations and attained tragic power, when he combined naturalistic drama with fateful characters and atmosphere in *Desire under the Elms*, produced in the fall of 1924.

A tragedy of passion involving the third wife of a New England farmer and his son by his deceased second wife, this work was altogether dynamic and grim. Suffering in this play was produced by strong passions and conflicts of will on the part of determined characters. And over the developing destiny of the fateful lovers, Eben and his stepmother Abbie, drawn irresistibly toward each other despite an initial conflict of interests, brood the trees, symbolic of natural fertility and mystery, of a flourishing New England farm. O'Neill, who belonged to a generation severely critical of Victorian, especially Puritan, morality, contrasted the passions of his youthful characters with the hardness and lovelessness of a Calvinist view of life. This is represented by the old farmer who has nothing but contempt for sensitive individuals like his son Eben — whom he takes for one of the world's weaklings —

and whose first and last trust is in the Old Testament God who tests men's strength with severe trials. Eben, who betrays his tyrannical father Ephraim Cabot, is engaged in Oedipal conflict with him; and the young stepmother Abbie, who married Ephraim because she sought security and coveted his farm, becomes tragically involved with her stepson when her suppressed hunger for love turns into reckless passion. *Desire under the Elms* held in solution O'Neill's critical view of his milieu and his interest in Freudian psychology as well as his tragic sense of life; and in this intense play he strained the boundaries of naturalistic drama until the play verged on melodrama when Abbie strangled her child in order to convince Eben that she had given herself to him out of love rather than out of a desire to deprive him of his heritage by producing a new heir to his father's farm. And in *Desire under the Elms*, as in earlier naturalistic plays, O'Neill also strained toward the estate of poetry with his symbols of fertility and an enveloping atmosphere of longing, loneliness, and lust. An imagination strengthened by a feeling for primitive severity in tone and characterization pervades this naturalistic treatment of a classic theme in which the Theseus is a lusty elderly farmer, the Hippolytus a mother-fixated son and jealous stepson, and the Phaedra a former household drudge with an ambition to secure her future as the inheritor of a thriving farm. If *Desire under the Elms* lacks the elevation it nevertheless possesses the strength of classic tragedy. If its stream of action is muddied by Freudian details of characterization in the portrayal of Eben, it nevertheless proceeds with mounting energy toward its destination, reflecting in its course the wind-swept landscape of the human soul. In any case, nothing comparable to this work in power derived from a sense of tragic character and situation had been achieved by the American theater in the hundred and fifty years of its history.

A more complacent playwright than O'Neill would have been

content with this achievement and endeavored to repeat it. Not so O'Neill, who did not give the American stage another naturalistic adaptation of classic subject matter until the Theatre Guild production of *Mourning Becomes Electra* in 1931. The plays that followed *Desire under the Elms* were *The Fountain*, unsuccessfully produced in December 1925 at the Greenwich Village Theatre, and *The Great God Brown*, presented at the same theater in January 1926. They represent O'Neill's strivings to enrich the American drama with styles radically different from the naturalistic — namely, the romantic, the symbolist, and the expressionistic.

The effort started earlier, in fact, with the production of *The Emperor Jones* in November 1920, and some seven months later with *Gold*, an expanded version of the one-acter *Where the Cross Is Made*. The first production was decidedly auspicious, the second inauspicious; the first virtually introduced expressionism into the American theater, the second inaugurated O'Neill's ventures into symbolist-romantic drama with which he succeeded only once — and but moderately even then — when the Theatre Guild produced *Marco Millions* in 1928. In the contrived and awkwardly written melodrama *Gold*, a sea captain is driven mad by his lust for gold, contracted on a desert island when, crazed by thirst, he thought he found a treasure trove. Its successor in the romantic style, *The Fountain*, fared scarcely better with the overextended story of the legendary search of Ponce de Leon for the Fountain of Youth which becomes obsessive until he finally realizes that "there is no gold but love." Only great dramatic poetry, which O'Neill was never to write, could have fulfilled his intentions, for it was his ambition here to attain exultation and not the "morbid realism" with which he considered himself unduly taxed. He was to return to this striving for verbal ecstasy with somewhat more success in the romantic scenes of *Marco Millions* but with generally turgid results in *Lazarus Laughed*, a boldly and nobly conceived drama in which the resurrected Lazarus teaches man to laugh at death.

Failure in romantic and symbolist drama could not, however, deter the playwright from seeking other means than realism for giving form to his vision of life and his aspirations for significant artistry. O'Neill was determined to enlarge the techniques of his playwriting, and this determination was sustained by a genuine need in his case to find suitable methods for expressing insights and attitudes for which realistic play structure seemed to him patently inadequate. Restiveness was only a secondary motive in O'Neill's case. European example, especially that of Strindberg, was a strong influence; his associates Macgowan and Jones had written enthusiastic and provocative reports on the European avant-garde in books and articles. But it was not direct example that influenced him. (He claimed to have had no knowledge of German expressionism when he conceived his first expressionist plays.) It was not theory but a felt belief in the potentialities of non-naturalistic drama that motivated O'Neill in the series of expressionistic experiments that started with the Provincetown Players productions of *The Emperor Jones* and *The Hairy Ape* in 1920 and 1922 respectively and continued, with a variety of modifications, in *All God's Chillun Got Wings* in 1924, in *The Great God Brown* in 1926, in *Strange Interlude* and *Lazarus Laughed* in 1928, and as late as 1934 in *Days without End*, a drama of a split personality played by two different actors. It was a personal pressure that dominated these plays and the statement of principles he set down for playwriting when he drafted the program note on Strindberg for the Provincetown Players production of *Spook Sonata*, which he co-produced: ". . . it is only by means of some form of 'super-naturalism' that we may express in the theater what we comprehend intuitively of that self-defeating self-obsession which is the discount we moderns have to pay for the loan of life. The old 'naturalism' — or 'realism' if you prefer . . . — no longer applies. It represents our Fathers' daring aspirations toward self-recognition by holding the family kodak up to ill-nature. But to us their old audacity is blague; we have taken too many snapshots of each other in every graceless position; we have endured too much from the banality of surfaces."

The first product of his reaching out for expressive form was *The Emperor Jones*, in which he dealt with the flight of a Caribbean Negro dictator from his aroused victims, a subject suggested to him by Haitian history, which he transformed into a succession of scenes of panic. In these vignettes, the man fleeing through the jungle is plagued by recollected events from his private past such as his slaying of a prison guard, his meager knowledge of racial history, and his superstitious fears and savage rituals.

Impacted into this drama of a frustrated escape and the influence of atavism was a powerful sense of theatricality which expressed itself most effectively in the incessant beat of tom-toms while the rebellious natives made magic and cast a silver bullet with which to destroy him, since he had fostered the belief that no other sort of bullet could harm him. O'Neill, having read accounts of Congo ritual, was impressed by the suggestive power of relentlessly repeated rhythms of the drum, "how it starts at a normal pulse and is slowly intensified until the heartbeat of everyone present corresponds to the frenzied beat of the drum." He asked himself, "How would this sort of thing work on an audience in a theater?" The question was quickly answered by the suspense and tension built up in the audience and the conclusive success of the play, which was also revived some years later with the celebrated Paul Robeson filling the role originally created by another gifted Negro actor, Charles Gilpin. (Later, the play was turned into an effective opera by Louis Gruenberg.) O'Neill's success with *The Emperor Jones* was dual: it was an original play — virtually a

18

dramatic monologue without intermissions in which fantasy cut across reality and the subjectivity of the protagonist was converted into objective reality for the mesmerized audience; and it was a play in which the wordless sequences were no less expressive than spoken dialogue.

The Emperor Jones was a tour de force of imaginative theater. It was followed by an even more exciting and certainly more provocative expressionistic drama, *The Hairy Ape*, which was somewhat baffling in meaning yet also richer and more complex in action and symbolization than *The Emperor Jones*. On the surface, the play was a series of vignettes dramatizing the bewilderment of a powerful stoker, Yank, when his naive confidence in brute power is shaken, and his desperate efforts to find a place for himself in the world (*"to belong,"* as he puts it); on a more sophisticated level, Yank's fate expressed man's search for the meaning of his life and his alienation in the universe. Its larger, metaphysical and not readily transparent meaning was more clearly defined by O'Neill himself in an interview published in the *New York Herald Tribune* of November 16, 1924. Yank, it was plain, was not merely a portrait based on O'Neill's memory of a rough and powerful stoker whose acquaintance he had made in Jimmy-the-Priest's New York waterfront dive, but an intellectual concept of man's alienation in an indifferent universe. He was a symbol, as O'Neill put it, of man "who has lost his old harmony with nature, the harmony which he used to have as an animal and has not yet acquired in a spiritual way." The public, O'Neill complained, saw only the baffled stoker, not the symbol; yet "the symbol makes the play either important or just another play."

As O'Neill went on to explain, Yank with his narrow spirit and limited intelligence is incapable of achieving any really developed humanity, even though no longer content with his previous animal-like status. He strikes out but blindly and in vain

19

against a reality he cannot affect or even comprehend: "Yank can't go forward, and so he tries to go back," as O'Neill put it. "This is what his shaking hands with the gorilla [in the last scene, set "in the monkey house at the Zoo"] meant. But he can't go back to 'belonging' either. The gorilla kills him."

O'Neill concluded that he had dramatized a universal theme: "The subject here is the same ancient one that always was and always will be the one subject for drama, and that is man and his struggle with his own fate. The struggle used to be with the gods, but is now with himself, his own past, his attempt 'to belong.'" It was to be O'Neill's primary theme in a series of plays that either failed or missed maximum effect to the degree to which in his impatience with realism he reduced characters to abstractions or harnessed them to metaphysical conceptions irreducible to concrete reality. In *The Hairy Ape* he succeeded in producing a powerful dramatic experience through the sheer vigor of the writing and the vibrancy of the action distributed in concise and visually arresting scenes. The fact, acknowledged by the playwright himself, that the public did not grasp the larger symbolic content did not greatly militate against the fascination and direct effect of the play. The ambiguities in it actually whetted the public's curiosity and, at the very least, served to differentiate *The Hairy Ape* from Zolaist "slice-of-life" naturalism.

O'Neill was less fortunate in a third expressionist experiment, *All God's Chillun Got Wings*, involving the marriage of a tarnished white girl and a devoted Negro lover. Here a metaphysical conception of fate seemed somewhat arbitrarily inserted into racial and psychological conflicts sufficiently immediate to make abstruseness a limitation rather than a valid extension of the drama. O'Neill dealt here with the subject of miscegenation and an ensuing Strindbergian duel of the sexes in the course of which the neurotically jealous Ella destroys her Negro husband's chances for a career and then, after going berserk and trying to kill him, lapses into remorseful dependency upon his forgiveness and devotion. Although O'Neill was not aroused especially by racial prejudice as a national problem and was resolutely disinclined to write problem plays, the story he had chosen in this play committed him to a non-metaphysical resolution of its tensions. Instead, he dissolved the substance of this provocative drama by placing the burden of guilt on God and fate instead of on society. "Will God forgive me, Jim?" Ella asks plaintively as she sinks into a state of childishness. Jim replies, "Maybe He can forgive what you've done to me; and maybe He can forgive what I've done to you; but I don't see how He's going to forgive — Himself." This rather irrelevant interchange was nevertheless intensely moving, as were Jim's later exclamation, even less relevant to the logic of the play, when he asks God to forgive his blasphemy: "Let this fire of burning suffering purify me of selfishness and make me worthy of the child You send me for the woman You take away!" and his response to his demented wife's plea that he play with her, when he cries out brokenheartedly: "Honey, Honey, I'll play right up to the gates of Heaven with you!" Once more O'Neill's intensity of feeling and uncanny sense of theater came to the rescue of his dramatic reasoning.

The same talents saved his next expressionistic experiment, *The Great God Brown*, from total disaster, leaving him with a flawed and overworked drama that was nevertheless impressive enough to win respect for his earnestness and his theatrical imagination while disappointing sociological critics. Here, too, O'Neill hit upon a recognizable social fact, which may be defined as the defeat of the artist in a materialistic and unsympathetic society, and here too he concentrated on private psychology and metaphysical intimations rather than sociology. Here, however, far from veering from the logic of his argument he pursued it so persistently that he pushed schematization to extremes of abstraction and weakened credibility and reality of character in the melodramatically snarled action of the drama. In no other play did O'Neill symbolize his theme so intensively. We must remember that his early Greenwich Village associates, especially Robert Edmond Jones, had been affected in their youth by the Symbolist school of literature, drama, and scenic design inspired by the semi-mystical aesthetic aims of Gordon Craig. With such avant-garde sanctions, O'Neill went confidently ahead in this play, splitting his characters into sharply contrasted personalities and even resorting to masks in order to represent the antinomies of the artistic and the pragmatically bourgeois temperaments. At one point the masks are interchanged for the purpose of dramatizing the seemingly placid bourgeois personality's envy and attempted incorporation of the artist. To effectuate his symbolizing intentions O'Neill virtually stopped at nothing in *The Great God Brown*, making it one of his boldest as well as most transparent theatrical experiments.

O'Neill had been driven once again to expressionist experiment and formal schematization by something deeper than a penchant for showmanship and a passion for experimentation. His generation, led by such rebels against the complacent materialism of a thriving middle-class society as Van Wyck Brooks, Sinclair Lewis, and H. L. Mencken, was keenly aware of the artist's isolation in such a milieu, which was either hostile or indifferent toward him, and American writers treated the subject variously in both realistic and fanciful novels, poems, and plays. O'Neill endeavored to treat it not farcically like George S. Kaufman and Marc Connelly in their Broadway expressionistic comedy *Beggar on Horseback*, but seriously; not urbanely and fancifully as did James Branch Cabell in *Jurgen* and other novels, but tragically; not realistically like Lewis in *Main Street* and *Babbitt*, but imaginatively. Primarily he was interested, as usual, in inner tensions and the drama of the soul, and it was to this end that he invented the use of masks to accentuate conflicts and changes in individuals and, in the last part of the play, to visualize a *transfer* of personality from one character to another. For some kinds of modern plays, O'Neill, who found it necessary to abandon the use of masks later on (notably in *Mourning Becomes Electra*), was at least temporarily convinced that the mask was the solution for expressing, as he put it in an essay on the subject, "those profound hidden conflicts of the mind which the probings of psychology continue to disclose." What, after all, were the new psychological insights of the age "but a study in masks" or "an exercise in unmasking"?

Troubled by the difficulty of communicating his meaning even with the device of the mask, O'Neill took pains to explicate his play in a newspaper article in the February 13, 1926, issue of the *New York Evening Post*. His chief character, Dion Anthony, represented in his dividedness the conflict between "the creative pagan acceptance of life," symbolized by Dionysus, constantly at war with the "masochistic, life-denying spirit of Christianity," symbolized by St. Anthony. The struggle resulted "in mutual exhaustion — creative joy in life for life's sake frustrated, rendered abortive, distorted by morality [O'Neill had in mind chiefly the puritanical morality of American society] from Pan into Satan, into a Mephistopheles mocking himself in order to feel alive." Perhaps Faust or, rather, Faust-Mephistopheles would have been a better choice of name, because O'Neill's heroine Margaret, Dion Anthony's long-suffering wife, was the playwright's image of the Marguerite of Goethe's *Faust*, "the eternal girl-woman with a virtuous simplicity of instinct, properly oblivious to everything but the means to her end of maintaining the race." Continuing his pattern of analogies, O'Neill made the prostitute Cybel, to whom his hero resorts for comfort and counsel, "the Earth Mother doomed to segregation as a pariah in a world of unnatural laws, but patronized by her segregators, who are thus themselves the first victims of their laws" (O'Neill's direct attack on puritanical hypocrisy); and Dion's friend, rival, and employer Brown stands for "the visionless demi-god of our new materialistic myth," inwardly "empty and resourceless," who builds his life with "exterior things" and moves uncreatively in "superficial preordained social grooves." The peripety at the end which conduces to confusion in the play consists of Brown's theft of the dying Dion's mask, which symbolizes his effort to appropriate the creativity energy he had envied in Dion. But despite believing that in stealing Dion's mask he has gained the power to create, he has actually possessed himself only of "that creative power made self-destructive by complete frustration"; and, says O'Neill, the "devil of mocking doubt makes short work of him" — a provocative idea for which O'Neill unfortunately found an incredibly melodramatic plot rather than a simple objective correlative. Despite this, the play ran nearly a year in 1926. One reason was probably the dramatic fascination of the novel and atmospherically enriched action. Another and simpler reason surely was the intensity of Dion's anguish as man and artist.

The Great God Brown, which exemplifies so much of O'Neill's striving for personal expression that it became his favorite play, was its author's most "successful" failure not merely in practical but also in dramatic and poetic terms. *Marco Millions*, which followed it some two years later, was pallid by comparison. O'Neill's animus against materialistic society led him to write a sardonic comedy on the career of Marco Polo, who turned rapidly into a philistine impervious to beauty and romance despite his travels in the wondrous East of Kublai Khan and the love of Princess Kukachin, the Khan's granddaughter. The playwright proved to be too heavy-handed and repetitive, making his point long before the conclusion and overextending the play in performance with his quasi-poetic rhetoric and requirements of spectacle. A lighter touch and a swifter pace, as well as greater verbal and situational inventiveness, were needed to realize its potentialities as satiric comedy. *Marco Millions* has its felicitous passages and telling moments. It cannot be written off as a total loss in the unfolding of its author's talent. But it cannot be considered a major or consistently absorbing work.

A return to his metaphysical vein in *Lazarus Laughed* led him into the blind alley of reiterative pseudo-philosophy from which he emerged too rarely to make this huge and unwieldy drama much more than an enormous spectacle strung upon a slender thread of plot and, despite its abundant rhetoric, a subliterary ritualistic effusion. In any case, this work was more suitable for outdoor pageantry than for the ordinary stage. Its chief interest lies in the variety of theatrical means — masks, choruses, crowds, choreographic movement, and other visual effects — O'Neill's stage-struck imagination could muster in the service of an idea. It could be said that on the level of show business, the son of the star-actor of *Monte Cristo* never quite left the spectacular romantic theater his father had turned into a livelihood; and that on the level of "art," he remained attached at heart to "Wagnerianism" or the *mélange des genres* aesthetic of Richard Wagner that influenced the late nineteenth- and the early twentieth-century theater. Inspiring these aesthetic proclivities was an earnest effort in O'Neill to express a tension that all the bohemian sophistication of the 1920's in America had been unable to allay or repress. It derived from the loss of religious faith that was traumatic in the case of the scion of an American Irish-Catholic family, and he was inwardly compelled to dwell upon the loss very much like his great Irish contemporary James Joyce.

O'Neill was aware of the possibility of pursuing substitutes and dramatized the search for them throughout his career. In *Lazarus Laughed* he temporarily found or thought he found an ersatz religion consisting of a mystical denial of death. It provided a doctrine of salvation by affirmation that was vastly more rhetorical than substantial. In *Dynamo*, his next engagement with the problem of faith, which had an unsuccessful though (largely thanks to the scenic genius of Theatre Guild designer Lee Simonson) visually stunning production early in 1929, he dramatized the substitution of machine-worship after his hero's renunciation of the puritanical faith of his fathers. While watching a dynamo in operation turning the energy of Connecticut rivers into electricity, O'Neill had been impressed with it as a veritable image of the new god of the scientific age. In *Dynamo* it became the dominant symbol, a hydroelectric generator described as "huge and black, with something of a massive female idol about it, the exciter set on the main structure like a head with blank oblong eyes above a gross, rounded torso," and it inspired him to undertake the writing of a trilogy on faith he never completed after the failure of *Dynamo* on the professional stage.

The story of the play, more simple than credible, revolved around a Calvinistically reared young American, Reuben Light, who, upon falling in love with an atheistical neighbor's daughter Ada, becomes an atheist himself. In search of a new faith to replace the old, Reuben adopts the electric generator as the symbol of his belief in science, paralleling the "Virgin and the Dynamo" contrast aptly drawn by Henry Adams. He soon finds himself worshipping the new god with the same violence with which his forebears worshipped the Old Testament deity. "O Dynamo, who gives life to things," he cries, "hear my prayer! Grant me the miracle of your love!" Driven mad by his fanaticism, he kills Ada, who made him violate his vow of undivided loyalty to the dynamo, following which he immolates himself on the lethal machine. *Dynamo* was a greater credit to its intrepid author's ambition than to his taste and discretion, and discouraged by the poor reception of the play, O'Neill abandoned his plan to write "a trilogy that will dig at the roots of the sickness of today as I feel it — the death of an old God and the failure of science and materialism to give any satisfying new one for the surviving primitive religious instinct to find a meaning for life in, and to comfort its fears of death with."

Nevertheless he could not resist his need to return to the subject of faith and the conflict with skepticism, which he described as the "big" subject behind all the little subjects of plays and novels whenever an author is not merely "scribbling around on the surface of things." He returned to the theme but with rather dreary results in *Days without End*, which O'Neill's latter-day producing organization, the Theatre Guild, presented for a short Broadway run in 1934. This play is for the most part a lesson on the need to return to conventional religious faith, but it is doubtful that O'Neill himself ever regained such faith for more than a brief period. (It remains to be noted that in Dublin the play reaped considerably more success than in New York; the conventional religious ending, in which the divided hero John Loving loses his skeptical, diabolical alter ego at the foot of the cross, apparently appealed more strongly to the Irish than to Americans.)

Fortunately, O'Neill had started a return to modified realism and interest in character-drama some half a dozen years earlier with *Strange Interlude*, which became a great Theatre Guild success in the year 1928. Instead of dealing with metaphysical content and struggles over faith, O'Neill concerned himself here with character dissection and inner conflict. Whatever means he adopted in this play, his schematizations and his recourse to the

Elizabethan device of the "aside" on a scale never before attempted on the stage, served the author's sole objective of portraying a modern woman. O'Neill showed her being driven by the strange life-force in her bloodstream to unconventional relationships, and seeking multiple possession of men's lives before peace descends upon her at the end of the "strange interlude" of her premenopausal life-history. With many details drawn from contemporary manners (the mores of the "sophisticated" 1920's) and contemporary psychology (chiefly Freudian), *Strange Interlude* proved engrossing to its New York public throughout the greater part of the long procession of revelations and incidents. The play was in nine acts (in contrast to the usual three-act play), ran from 5:30 P.M. until past 11 save for an eighty-minute dinner interval, and traced the critical relationships of a small number of characters for nearly three decades. Above all the characters stood Nina, the attractive daughter of a possessive university professor, who lost her athlete lover in World War I, regretted not having consummated her love with him, and sought fulfillment in desperate promiscuity. Later, having married a man to whom she would not bear children after being warned by his mother that there was insanity in the family, she gave birth to a son by another man (the neurologist Darrell) but could not bring herself to leave her husband and never could reveal the boy's true parentage. It takes a husband, a lover, a family friend, and an illegitimate son to fill her womanly life while at full tide. Then, as the vital flood recedes, she loses her husband to death, her emotionally drained lover to science, and her athlete son to a girl of his own age. By then, however, a twilight calm is descending on the central figure of this novel in play form, in which a vital modern woman is observed from many angles and in many situations. The resulting portrait was drawn on the stage by the gifted and resourceful Lynn Fontanne with such conviction that no one was likely to look for hidden meanings while she held the stage, which she did most of the time.

As a matter of fact, there were no hidden meanings in the play; if anything, O'Neill was only too explicit in his spoken and especially his supposedly unspoken dialogue — that is, the asides with which the author outlined the true thoughts and sentiments of the characters at the risk of redundancy. There could well be two strongly contradictory opinions about the recourse to asides. The British theater historian Allardyce Nicoll deplored them as a "somewhat tedious and fundamentally undramatic elaboration of the quite worthy convention of the 'aside' into a pretentious artistic instrument." Others found much to approve in this type of "interior dialogue," which bore considerable resemblance to the stream-of-consciousness James Joyce employed in *Ulysses*. In the excellently paced Theatre Guild production of 1928, staged by the gifted director Philip Moeller with an incredibly apt and able cast, there was little cause for complaint except for the decline of interest in the last two acts. In a highly professional New York revival given about a third of a century later by the Actors Studio Theatre, the negative opinion was more or less vindicated. Even then, however, *Strange Interlude* impressed the majority of reviewers and playgoers as a weighty experiment and, more than that, as a wide-ranging human document. What rigorous criticism was tempted to dismiss in that document as mere cliché overinsistently communicated was redeemed by effective confrontations of the chief characters and by the substantiality of Nina Leeds as a veritable incarnation of *das Ewig-Weibliche*. Nina, whose grosser and more elemental ancestress may be said to be Wedekind's Lulu, is a sort of Social Register earth goddess who encompasses during her "strange interlude" the functions of daughter, wife, mother, mistress, and superwoman whom all men find attractive and whose needs no single man is capable of fulfilling, although it is surmised that the untimely lost lover, Gordon, might have been able to satisfy them. Both as a character study and as a dramatic novel *Strange Interlude* commanded the interest of a large public grateful for an exacting and unconventional drama. And its augmented realism was sufficiently successful to direct its author back to the paths of realism he had followed rewardingly in the early sea and waterfront plays.

This was notably apparent in his *Mourning Becomes Electra* trilogy, when he domesticated or "naturalized" Greek legend and its various treatments by the Greek tragic poets. This was truly an enormous undertaking worthy of his ambition to treat significant themes and apply to them the insights and idiom of his own age. Although he employed formal elements in this work such as a truncated chorus and mask-like facial expressions, these did not undercut the fundamentally naturalistic character of the work but merely punctuated and magnified it. Turning to the Orestean theme treated by Aeschylus and his successors, O'Neill localized it in New England immediately after the conclusion of the Civil War (instead of the Trojan War) in 1865, and translated and paralleled it in terms of the American environment of that period. The scion of a wealthy mercantile family, General Ezra Mannon, the Agamemnon of *Mourning Becomes Electra*, returns from the Civil War to learn that his alienated wife Christine (the Clytemnestra of O'Neill's treatment) has been unfaithful to him with the seafaring Adam Brant from a rival branch of the family, and to be poisoned by her when he seeks a reconciliation. In the second part of O'Neill's trilogy, as in *The Libation Bearers* of Aeschylus and the *Electra*'s of Sophocles and Euripides, the Electra character whom O'Neill calls Lavinia and her brother, O'Neill's Orestes named Orin, avenge their father's death by killing their mother's lover Adam Brant, the Aegisthus of the modern play, whereupon the mother commits suicide. In the third of the trilogy, the burden of guilt rests heavily on the son, although unlike the Orestes of the Greek plays, he did not directly murder his mother. Orin is virtually mad, and so dependent on his sister Lavinia that he won't allow her to marry anyone. At this point O'Neill whipped up the action into a rather melodramatic frenzy with his Electra driving his Orestes to suicide, following which she is so overwhelmed with remorse that she renounces all possibilities of happiness, shutting herself up forever with her conscience in the mansion of the ill-fated Mannons.

The power of this work communicated itself instantly on the stage in the memorable Philip Moeller production of the year 1931 for the Theatre Guild. It had a neoclassical-colonial setting by Robert Edmond Jones and featured the veteran actress Nazimova in the role of Christine and Alice Brady (succeeded by Judith Anderson) in the part of Lavinia. But there was more to the play than the transcription of Greek matter into American terms. O'Neill, it is true, did not differ from the Greek tragedians in concerning himself with Fate and the working out of the family curse, the "domestic Ate," in the story of a New England Brahmin family. But it was his intention to go much further and translate fate into modern terms, an enterprise already started before him by the late nineteenth-century naturalists who found an equivalent for the Greek idea of fate in their rudimentary scientific concepts of determinism by heredity and environment. Locating the determinism more directly in the human psyche, O'Neill adopted the Freudian emphasis upon the sexual instinct, especially the much publicized Oedipus complex. His Clytemnestra had been horrified on her wedding night by her husband's brutal sexuality (a case of the libido welling up from puritanical suppression) and subsequently felt alienated from the fruit of their union, Lavinia, thus alienating her daughter and making the girl excessively attached to her father, Mannon. She had lavished

31

possessive affection, however, on her second child, Orin, during her husband's absence when America waged war with Mexico, thus causing the son to be pathetically fixated on her. It is chiefly Oedipal resentment that pits the Electra of O'Neill's trilogy against his Clytemnestra, and it is Oedipal attachment that makes O'Neill's Orestes the tool of his sister's animosity, which results in his seeking out and killing Captain Adam Brant on his ship. Orin's act and Lavinia's provocation lead step by step then to his mother's suicide, his disturbed state of mind, his incestuous dependency on the sister (who has begun to resemble the mother she has destroyed), and his own death.

Schematization was carried too far in the play, but the Freudian interpretation produced intensely dramatic moments, especially in the mother-daughter conflict. Still, in resorting to psychoanalytical explanations and highlighting them in each of the three plays of the trilogy, O'Neill deprived his characters of tragic stature insofar as they became clinical cases, and this invited criticism from some quarters that O'Neill had written a case history rather than a tragedy. One could offer the defense that the characters and events as observed in the Theatre Guild production certainly *felt* tragic — at least until the excrescence of melodramatic action in the last part of the work. A better case could be made against the trilogy by those who noted the poverty of O'Neill's low-grade naturalistic dialogue, so distressingly at variance with the powerful passions and mounting action of the trilogy, so downright flat precisely when the language should have been made to soar, as in the scene in which Orin tells his mother that he has killed her lover:

CHRISTINE. (*stammers*) Orin! What kept you — ?

ORIN. We just met Hazel. She said you were terribly frightened at being alone here. That is strange — when you have the memory of Father for company!

CHRISTINE. You — you stayed all this time — at the Bradfords'?

ORIN. We didn't go to the Bradfords'.

CHRISTINE. (*stupidly*) You didn't go — to Blackridge?

ORIN. We took the train there but we decided to stay right on and go to Boston instead.

CHRISTINE. (*terrifiedly*) To — Boston — ?

ORIN. And in Boston we waited until the evening train got in. We met that train.

CHRISTINE. Ah!

ORIN. We had an idea you would take advantage of our being in Blackridge to be on it — and you were! And we followed you when you called on your lover in his cabin!

CHRISTINE. (*with a pitiful effort at indignation*) Orin! How dare you talk — ! (*Then brokenly*) Orin! Don't look at me like that! Tell me —

ORIN. Your lover! Don't lie! You've lied enough, Mother! I was on deck, listening! What would you have done if you had discovered me? Would you have gotten your lover to murder me, Mother? I heard you warning him against me! But your warning was no use!

CHRISTINE. (*chokingly*) What — ? Tell me — !

ORIN. I killed him!

CHRISTINE. (*with a cry of terror*) Oh — oh! I knew! (*Then clutching at* Orin) No — Orin! You — you're just telling me that — to punish me, aren't you? You said you loved me — you'd protect me — protect your mother — you couldn't murder — !

One expects less prosaic language from a master tragedian, which O'Neill narrowly missed becoming in this play.

The language and the heavy emphasis on incestuous feelings elicited unfavorable comment at first mostly in England and later in American literary circles, the most considered being perhaps Allardyce Nicoll's conclusion that "This is rather a magnificently presented case-study than a powerful tragic drama." O'Neill resented the allegation that he had borrowed his ideas, claiming that he knew enough about human nature to have written the play without having ever heard of Freud and Jung. But O'Neill had himself imposed restraints on his endeavor to write a modern high tragedy by domesticating the Orestean legend to the point of restricting his dialogue to naturalistic commonplaceness, and by asking himself (in his preparatory notes to *Mourning Becomes Electra*) whether it was possible to "get modern psychological approximation of Greek sense of fate into such a play." His play is an affirmative answer which, nevertheless, leaves unanswered the larger question O'Neill did *not* ask himself — namely, whether modern dramatic vision needs to be limited, or is actually exhausted, by "psychological approximation."

Some necessity of art and personal expression, then, kept O'Neill moving back to realistic drama as the style of writing by which his reputation would stand or fall. This led him to yield to psychopathology and lapse into sunless Gothic melodrama in *Mourning Becomes Electra*. It also led him, two years later, to the pleasant alternative of producing the genial genrepainting of *Ah, Wilderness!*, a family comedy set in a small Connecticut city at the beginning of the century. A nostalgic comedy of recollection, it revolves around a bright and spirited adolescent who has his first and luckily harmless fling at low life when jilted by the daughter of a parochial father, who disapproves of the boy's penchant for the "pagan" poet Swinburne. The boy's understanding and ever-smiling father, who is the local newspaper publisher, straightens everything out to his son's satisfaction, and to the gratification of playgoers pleased at meeting O'Neill for once without his tragic mask. The popular star George M. Cohan, playing the newspaper publisher, toured this comedy of reconciliation across the nation without adding substantially to O'Neill's reputation or altering it for admirers, who cherished their memory of him as a singularly sultry dramatist. Today, *Ah, Wilderness!* falls into proper perspective as one of the most attractive of American domestic comedies — nothing less, and nothing more. For the author him-self it was only a brief holiday from his most persistent memories, which were normally bleak, and from the contemporary world, about which he never felt particularly cheerful. That it repre-sented only a vacation from a gloomy view of *la condition humaine* was to become evident in his last plays, first brought to the stage many years later while O'Neill was leading a life of mental and physical torment and, in the case of several of his plays (*Long Day's Journey into Night, A Touch of the Poet*, the one-acter *Hughie*, and *More Stately Mansions*), after his death in 1953.

More than a decade — twelve years, to be exact — elapsed be-tween the middle and last periods of O'Neill's career. These were years of isolation during which he planned and wrote plays he withheld from the stage and did not publish. Illness ham-pered him and depression over the state of the world, which was veering rapidly toward a global war, immobilized him and kept him virtually bedridden at times. As late as 1946, he still felt that it would require strong efforts on his part to recover enough confidence in the worth of literary labor to start writing again. In a press interview he declared that "the war has thrown me com-pletely off base. . . . I have to get back to a sense of writing be-ing worthwhile." Morosely, he added, "In fact, I'd have to pre-tend." It was not a period to encourage optimism, and there was none forthcoming from O'Neill as he brooded on the past that prepared the way for the dreadful present while at work on a tre-mendous cycle of plays tracing the tragic history of an Amer-ican family from colonial times to his own, destroying some of his completed drafts and leaving other planned plays unwritten or un-finished.

Shortly after the conclusion of World War II, it became possi-ble for him to entertain prospects for new productions and to al-low the publication of two new plays, *The Iceman Cometh*,

written in 1939, and *A Moon for the Misbegotten*, completed
in 1943. Both were to a degree memory plays, the first dealing
with the period of his waterfront days at Jimmy-the-Priest's dive,
the second with the broken life of his alcoholic brother James.
But the mordancy of both plays derived not from memories (the
autobiographical elements were thoroughly transformed) but
from a strong and vivid sense of man's private and public failure,
which the recently concluded holocaust and the growing materialism of the world only served to confirm. In an interview he gave
to the press in September 1946, on the occasion of the Broadway
opening of *The Iceman Cometh* by the Theatre Guild, O'Neill
held out little hope for man. He included in his indictment
his own nation, which had but recently emerged the victor and
the champion of humanity from a second world war. "I'm going
on the theory," he declared, "that the United States, instead of
being the most successful country in the world, is the greatest failure." His country had been given more resources than any other,
but while moving ahead rapidly it had not acquired any real roots
because its main idea appeared to be "that everlasting game of
trying to possess your own soul by the possession of something
outside it." He included the rest of the world in his indictment.
If the human was so "damned stupid" that in two thousand
years it had not learned to heed the Biblical admonition
against gaining the whole world but losing one's own soul, then
it was time humanity were "dumped down the nearest drain" and
the ants were given a chance to succeed where men had failed.

The Iceman Cometh, which the Theatre Guild produced with
only moderate success but which was later revived with great success, proved to be one of O'Neill's most powerful as well
as most pessimistic plays. Bearing considerable resemblance to
Maxim Gorki's turn-of-the-century naturalistic classic *The Lower
Depths* (both plays are set in a cheap boardinghouse for the dis-

reputable and the derelict, and both show man trying to subsist on illusory hopes), *The Iceman Cometh* nevertheless presents a radically different view from that entertained by the Russian author who had stood at the dawn of the twentieth century and shared its optimism. O'Neill expressed no hope for men at all, and therefore considered illusion to be the necessary anodyne and death a welcome release for bedeviled mankind. In Harry Hope's saloon, life's exiles and failures lead a besotted and befuddled existence and subsist on hopes of recovering their lost status. Most of them are reasonably happy until their drinking companion, the flashy traveling salesman Hickey, shows up for one of his periodic drinking bouts. Instead of joining in the expected revels, however, he is bent upon making them renounce their illusions and face the truth about themselves, which is that they no longer have anything to hope for. Accepting his challenge, at last, that they leave the saloon and proceed to accomplish the restitution of reputation and position with which they have long deluded themselves, they sally forth, but only to return, one by one, frightened and dispirited. Nothing feels right anymore, and even the liquor in the saloon has lost its savor and has no effect on them. Contentment returns to them only after Hickey's revelation that he has murdered his long-suffering wife who persisted in believing in his eventual reformation as the only way to free her from the misery of loving him, although he has also hated her for her infinite trust and forbearance. ("I couldn't forgive her for forgiving me," says Hickey. "I even caught myself hating her for making me hate myself so much.")

They derive reassurance from the conviction that Hickey, who has given himself up to the police, is stark mad, and relapse into their comforting illusions. The liquor begins to have an effect on them again, and all is well with them once more, so far as they know or care. The one exception is Larry, the disenchanted radical,

37

who also turns out to be the only convert the miserable Hickey made, for Larry is the only one who really grasped Hickey's meaning when Hickey called for the abandonment of illusions as the only way of attaining peace. The death of illusion is the end of life, death, "the Iceman," being the sole possible release. For, as Larry has said earlier about men's dependence on false hopes, "the lie of a pipe dream is what gives life to the whole misbegotten mad lot of us, drunk or sober." Larry, in fact, performs one act of kindness at once; he persuades a miserable youth, who has betrayed his anarchist mother to the police, to put an end to his inner torment by committing suicide.

Rich in detail, complex in contrivance yet seemingly natural, naturalistic in speech and situation yet also somewhat symbolic and grotesque, *The Iceman Cometh* looms large in the O'Neill canon. Even its prolixity has redeeming qualities; Hickey's confessional speech, which lasts some fifteen minutes on the stage, constitutes gripping theater. Its defects are the corrigible one of repetitiveness, some of which can be removed without injury to the play, the slight but embarrassing one of some banality of expression (as in the overuse of outmoded slang and the jejune phrase "pipe dreams" for false hopes), and the intrinsic one of spiritual torpor that derives from its author's persistent philosophy of negation.

The failure of O'Neill's next production, *A Moon for the Misbegotten,* which was withdrawn after its out-of-town tryout in February and March 1947, marked the end of its author's active participation in the theater. *The Iceman Cometh,* which opened in New York on September 2, 1946, was the last of O'Neill's plays to be seen on Broadway in his lifetime.

During his final years O'Neill was stricken with an obscure degenerative disease which made writing and finally even locomotion extremely difficult, although his mind remained clear. His

38

third wife, actress Carlotta Monterey, whom he married in 1929, was his nurse during these years, and for long periods they lived in virtual seclusion, in Marblehead, Massachusetts, and later Boston. He had become wholly estranged from the children, Shane and Oona, of his second marriage, to Agnes Boulton. (O'Neill had been so angered by Oona's marriage, at eighteen, to Charlie Chaplin, who was the same age as O'Neill himself, that he never again — according to his wife Carlotta — mentioned her name.) His older son, Eugene, Jr., born of his short-lived first marriage to Kathleen Jenkins, committed suicide in 1950.

Three years after O'Neill's death, and a decade after *The Iceman Cometh* opened, his posthumous career on Broadway began brilliantly, with the José Quintero production of *Long Day's Journey into Night*, which had Fredric March, Florence Eldridge, Jason Robards, Jr., and Bradford Dillman in the main parts. This opening, on November 7, 1956, repeated the earlier triumph of the play's world première in Swedish at the Royal Dramatic Theatre in Stockholm on February 10, 1956. (In 1945 O'Neill had stipulated that *Long Day's Journey into Night*, which has strong autobiographical overtones, should be sealed for twenty-five years after his death. But Carlotta O'Neill, as his literary executrix, released the play for both publication and production, saying that her husband had changed his mind after the death of Eugene, Jr., at whose request O'Neill had originally withheld the play.)

In *Long Day's Journey into Night*, in many respects a simple naturalistic family drama, there were no plot contrivances, no "well-made" play intrigues, but only uncommonly moving revelations of character and human relations. These came in the wake of closely connected tensions and conflicts shattering to the young man, actually the young O'Neill, who is patently the transcriber of the events of the play. Were it not for the prosaic quality of the dialogue and the extreme length of the work, there could be no doubt whatsoever that it is a twentieth-century dramatic master-piece.

Long Day's Journey into Night brought O'Neill back to his real forte, and that of most American playwrights — plain, honest realism of character and situation. For all that, and despite his laboring of some points (finesse was never one of his virtues), O'Neill could not be charged fairly with commonplace obvious-ness. He was subtle in his own way in noting the complexity of the young hero's somewhat avaricious and penny-pinching actor-father, his mother too frightened of life to be able to give up the drug habit, and his demon-driven alcoholic brother. *Long Day's Journey into Night* is perhaps the modern theater's outstand-ing dramatization of the ambivalences omnipresent in the human species. This alone would have given authenticity and depth to the play, which O'Neill managed to convey with much dramat-ic skill in a crescendo of revelations and even with some delight-ful humor, as in the scene in which the father tries to contradict the charge of miserliness by turning on all the lights in the par-lor and then cautiously turning them out again. A forgiving spirit hovered over O'Neill when he came to write his chef-d'oeuvre (in 1940, sixteen years before its production), and his reward was the favorable response of even those members of the new genera-tion who had found little to praise and much to blame in the playwright's earlier plays. For them, moreover, there could be spe-cial merit in the analytical, unsentimental insight that accom-panied the compassion. The young O'Neill, who manifests a poet's sensitivity and a literary bent, is shown acquiring a painful understanding of life's ironies, which in the mature O'Neill's own case is not a jaundiced view of humanity but the tragic sense of life for which he became noted.

After *Long Day's Journey into Night*, the New York production of *A Moon for the Misbegotten*, which opened about half a year later (in May 1957), was bound to seem anticlimactic despite the services of the gifted British actress Wendy Hiller in the role of an oversized farm girl who tries to bestow her love on a guilt-laden alcoholic lacking all capacity to receive, let alone return, it. Faulty in several respects, it was nevertheless another work of considerable depth and compassion, here presented largely in terms of grotesque comedy.

Also weak in some respects, *A Touch of the Poet* (which, although written in 1936, first opened on Broadway on October 2, 1958, about six months after the world première at the Royal Dramatic Theatre) is chiefly noteworthy for giving us an inkling of what its author had in mind for the dramatic cycle he had planned under the title of *A Tale of Possessors Self-Dispossessed* and abandoned. This play, the sole finished survivor of the project, dramatized the beginnings of the American family with which the cycle was to deal. Here the daughter of an Irish pretender to aristocratic status, Con Melody, reduced to keeping a pub near Boston, resolves to marry the poetical scion of a wealthy Brahmin family despite parental interference. The full significance of the play could not be established without reference to the nonexistent cycle, but its self-sufficient qualities were considerable. They were most evident in the character studies of a man who is dignified by his sense of distinction out of all proportion to his merits (he is a liar and often an inconsiderate one), his drudge of a wife who in understanding his proud spirit forgives all hurts, and his daughter Sara who scorns his pretensions but mourns for him as one dead when he renounces them.

Another play, *More Stately Mansions*, which was apparently to be the fourth in his eleven-play cycle and was to follow *A Touch of the Poet*, was retrieved from the O'Neill papers in Yale University's O'Neill Collection and produced in considerably shortened form by Dr. Karl Ragnar Gierow, the Royal Dramatic Theatre director who had staged productions of two other posthumous O'Neill works in Stockholm, in November 1962. The manuscript was revised for publication by Dr. Gierow and Donald Gallup, the curator of the O'Neill Collection at Yale. Since this version, released by the Yale University Press in 1964, was prepared from the Swedish acting script, it cannot be judged as an original O'Neill work; the original manuscript is more than twice as long as the published play. Whatever the favorable impression of the Swedish production, the published play may well strike a reader as decidedly scattered in effect. But it is plain that O'Neill wanted to indict the growth of materialism in the modern world. Con Melody's daughter Sara of *A Touch of the Poet* is here married to the young man, Simon Harford, she fancied. But her possessiveness and her rivalry with his equally possessive mother prove to be his undoing; the poet in him dies as he becomes a relentless materialist before breaking down mentally. O'Neill's old feeling for compulsive conflict is once more uppermost in this salvaged but rather inchoate drama, which has yet to be tested on the American stage.

Fortunately, there was one more posthumously published work of the final period that shows no decline or dispersion of O'Neill's power, the short two-character masterpiece *Hughie,* written in 1941 and published in 1959, the first of a projected series grimly entitled *By Way of Obit.* For the most part a monologue spoken by the "Broadway sport" Erie Smith to the night clerk of a shabby New York hotel in the late 1920's, *Hughie* is a tour de force that does not flag for a moment in revealing the emotional vacuity of the narrator and a deceased night clerk, Hughie, whom he used to fill with wonder at his inflated gambling exploits. Marvelously vivid and rhythmic dialogue that seems utterly authentic in its colloquialism and slang in this play recalls O'Neill's early achievements in the best sea-pieces of the *S. S. Glencairn* series.

42

Hughie is the last testament to O'Neill's prowess in naturalistic playwriting and to his lingering attachment, despite his success with oversized dramas, to the spare one-act play form with which he had first established his reputation as an authentic American playwright.

Nothing needs to be added perhaps to this critical chronicle of the efforts and achievements of the one American playwright whose place in the hierarchy of world dramatists seems as secure as any twentieth-century dramatist's can be. To his critics' justifiable impatience with his laboriousness the appropriate reply is that O'Neill is the *master* of massive dramatic assault. His power is not often separable from his repetitiveness or even verbosity. His sense of theater was so strong that more often than not his best plays, when well structured, proved to be considerably more effective on the stage than a literary reading of them could possibly suggest. His sense of drama was so rarely "posture" despite his not always trustworthy flair for theatricality that much of his work seems wrung from him rather than contrived or calculated. In a very real sense it is a testament to a uniquely tormented spirit that subsumed much of the twentieth century's dividedness and anguish, largely existential rather than topical. And while the penalty for his metaphysical concerns and brooding inwardness was often a quasi-philosophical windiness, the reward for his refusal to settle for small temporary satisfactions is an aura of greatness in the man and his labors, or, at the very least, a dark impressiveness not easily to be dismissed by dwelling on his verbal limitations. This much can be said, without fear of contradiction, of the man who, in the words of his publisher-friend Bennett Cerf, was "the first universally recognized world dramatist America produced" in some two centuries of theater in the Western hemisphere.

⤴ Selected Bibliography

Works of Eugene O'Neill

PLAYS

Thirst. Boston: Gorham Press, 1914. (This book contains three other one-act plays by O'Neill: *Warnings, Fog,* and *Recklessness*.)

Bound East for Cardiff. In *The Provincetown Plays: First Series*. New York: Frank Shay, 1916.

Before Breakfast. In *The Provincetown Plays: Third Series*. New York: Frank Shay, 1916.

The Moon of the Caribbees. New York: Boni and Liveright, 1919. (This book also contains other one-act plays: *In the Zone, Where the Cross Is Made, The Rope, The Long Voyage Home,* and *Ile*.)

Beyond the Horizon. New York: Boni and Liveright, 1920.

The Emperor Jones, Diff'rent, The Straw. New York: Boni and Liveright, 1921.

Gold. New York: Boni and Liveright, 1921.

The Hairy Ape, Anna Christie, The First Man. New York: Boni and Liveright, 1924.

Desire under the Elms. New York: Boni and Liveright, 1925.

The Great God Brown, The Fountain. New York: Boni and Liveright, 1926.

Marco Millions. New York: Boni and Liveright, 1927.

Lazarus Laughed. New York: Boni and Liveright, 1927.

Strange Interlude. New York: Boni and Liveright, 1928.

Dynamo. New York: Horace Liveright, 1929.

Mourning Becomes Electra. New York: Horace Liveright, 1931.

Ah, Wilderness! New York: Random House, 1933.

Days without End. New York: Random House, 1934.

The Iceman Cometh. New York: Random House, 1946.

The Lost Plays of Eugene O'Neill. New York: New Fathoms Publication, 1950. (Unauthorized publication of immature short plays which O'Neill did not wish to publish.)

A Moon for the Misbegotten. New York: Random House, 1952.

Long Day's Journey into Night. New Haven, Conn.: Yale University Press, 1956.

A Touch of the Poet. New Haven, Conn.: Yale University Press, 1957.

New Girl in Town. (A musical based on the play *Anna Christie*, with book by George Abbott and music and lyrics by Bob Merrill.) New York: Random House, 1958.

44

Hughie. New Haven, Conn.: Yale University Press, 1959.
Take Me Along. (A musical based on the play *Ah, Wilderness!*) New York: Random House, 1960.
More Stately Mansions. New Haven, Conn.: Yale University Press, 1964.
Ten Lost Plays. (Authorized Edition.) New York: Random House, 1964.

(It should be noted that several of O'Neill's plays were first published in periodicals: *The Long Voyage Home* in *Smart Set*, October 1917 issue; *Ile* in *Smart Set*, May 1918 issue; *The Moon of the Caribbees* in *Smart Set*, August 1918 issue; *The Dreamy Kid* in *Theatre Arts*, January 1920 issue; *The Emperor Jones* in *Theatre Arts*, January 1921 issue; *All God's Chillun Got Wings* in the *American Mercury*, February 1924 issue.)

OTHER WRITINGS

"Strindberg and Our Theater," *Provincetown Playbill*, No. 1, Season of 1923–24. (Reprinted in Helen Deutsch and Stella Hanau, *The Provincetown: A Story of the Theatre.* New York: Farrar and Rinehart, 1931. Pp. 191–93.)
"Are the Actors to Blame?" *Provincetown Playbill*, No. 1, Season of 1925–26. (Reprinted in Deutsch and Hanau, *The Provincetown.* Pp. 197–98.)
"Memoranda on Masks," *American Spectator*, November 1932.

COLLECTED EDITIONS

The Complete Plays of Eugene O'Neill, with brief notes by the author. Wilderness Edition, 12 volumes. New York: Scribner's, 1934–35.
The Plays of Eugene O'Neill. Lifetime Library Edition, 3 volumes. New York: Random House, 1946.

CURRENT AMERICAN REPRINTS

Ah, Wilderness! and Two Other Plays: All God's Chillun Got Wings and Beyond the Horizon. New York: Modern Library (Random House). $2.45.
The Emperor Jones, edited by Max J. Herzberg. New York: Appleton-Century-Crofts. $.95.
The Emperor Jones, Anna Christie, and *The Hairy Ape.* New York: Modern Library. $2.45.
The Iceman Cometh. New York: Vintage (Random House). $1.45.
A Touch of the Poet. New Haven, Conn.: Yale University Press. $1.25.
Long Day's Journey into Night. New Haven, Conn.: Yale University Press. $1.45.
The Long Voyage Home: Seven Plays of the Sea. (Includes *The Moon of the Caribbees, Bound East for Cardiff, The Long Voyage Home, In the Zone, Ile, Where the Cross Is Made, The Rope.*) New York: Modern Library. $1.95.
Lost Plays of Eugene O'Neill. New York: Citadel. $1.50.

More Stately Mansions. New Haven, Conn.: Yale University Press. $1.95. (Abridgement.)

Nine Plays. New York: Modern Library. $2.95.

Six Short Plays: The Dreamy Kid, Before Breakfast, Diff'rent, Welded, The Straw, Gold. New York: Vintage. $1.65.

Three Plays: Desire under the Elms, Strange Interlude, Mourning Becomes Electra. New York: Vintage. $1.65.

Bibliographies

"The Theatre of O'Neill," *Greenwich Playbill* (program of O'Neill's *The Fountain*), No. 3, Season of 1925–26. (A list of plays, including manuscripts lost or destroyed by O'Neill.)

Sanborn, Ralph, and Barrett H. Clark. *A Bibliography of the Works of Eugene O'Neill.* New York: Random House, 1931.

Sanborn, Ralph. "Check-List of the First Publication of the Plays of Eugene O'Neill," in Barrett H. Clark's *Eugene O'Neill: The Man and His Plays.*

Bryer, Jackson R. "Forty Years of O'Neill Criticism: A Selected Bibliography," *Modern Drama*, 4:196–216 (September 1961).

Miller, Jordan Y. *Eugene O'Neill and the American Critic: A Summary and Bibliographical Checklist.* London: Archon Books, 1962.

Critical and Biographical Studies

BOOKS AND PAMPHLETS

Bentley, Eric R. *In Search of Theater.* New York: Knopf, 1953. Pp. 233–47.

———. "Introduction to O'Neill," in *Major Writers of America*, edited by Perry Miller. New York: Harcourt, Brace, and World, 1962. Vol. 2, pp. 557–75.

Block, Anita. *The Changing World in Plays and Theatre.* Boston: Little, Brown, 1939. Pp. 137–93.

Boulton, Agnes. *Part of a Long Story.* Garden City, N.Y.: Doubleday, 1958.

Bowen, Croswell. *The Curse of the Misbegotten.* New York: McGraw-Hill, 1959.

Brown, John Mason. *Letters from Greenroom Ghosts.* New York: Viking, 1934.

———. *Seeing More Things.* New York: Whittlesey House, 1948. Pp. 257–65.

———. *Still Seeing Things.* New York: McGraw-Hill, 1950. Pp. 185–95.

Brustein, Robert. *The Theatre of Revolt.* Boston: Little, Brown, 1964. Pp. 319–60.

Buck, Philo Melvin, Jr. *Directions in Contemporary Literature.* New York: Oxford University Press, 1942. Pp. 125–47.

Clark, Barrett H. *Eugene O'Neill: The Man and His Plays.* Revised edition. New York: Dover, 1947.

Cargill, Oscar, N. Bryllion Fagin, William J. Fisher, editors. *O'Neill and His Plays*. New York: New York University, 1961.

Downer, Alan S. *Fifty Years of American Drama, 1900–1950*. Chicago: Regnery, 1951. Pp. 64–70, 92–97.

Engel, Edwin A. *The Haunted Heroes of Eugene O'Neill*. Cambridge, Mass.: Harvard University Press, 1953.

Falk, Doris V. *Eugene O'Neill and the Tragic Tension: An Interpretive Study of the Plays*. New Brunswick, N.J.: Rutgers University Press, 1958.

Gagey, Edmond M. *Revolution in American Drama*. New York: Columbia University Press, 1947. Pp. 39–70.

Gassner, John. *Masters of the Drama*. Revised edition. New York: Dover, 1954. Pp. 639–61, 735–36.

———. *Theatre at the Crossroads*. New York: Holt, Rinehart, and Winston, 1960. Pp. 66–76.

———. *The Theatre in Our Times*. New York: Crown, 1954. Pp. 249–66.

———, editor. *O'Neill: A Collection of Critical Essays*. Englewood Cliffs, N.J.: Prentice-Hall, 1964.

Geddes, Virgil. *The Melodramadness of Eugene O'Neill*. Brookfield Pamphlets No. 4. Brookfield, Conn.: Brookfield Players, 1934.

Gelb, Arthur, and Barbara Gelb. *O'Neill*. New York: Harper, 1962.

Helburn, Theresa. *A Wayward Quest*. Boston: Little, Brown, 1960. Pp. 256–80.

Hicks, Granville. *The Great Tradition*. New York: Macmillan, 1933. Pp. 207–56.

Kerr, Walter. *Pieces at Eight*. New York: Simon and Schuster, 1957. Pp. 117–49.

Krutch, Joseph Wood. *The American Drama since 1918*. New York: Random House, 1939. Pp. 73–133.

Lamm, Martin. *Modern Drama*, translated by Karin Elliott. New York: Philosophical Library, 1953. Pp. 315–33.

Langner, Lawrence. *The Magic Curtain*. New York: Dutton, 1951. Pp. 228–42, 397–409.

Moses, Montrose J., and John Mason Brown. *The American Theatre as Seen by Its Critics, 1752–1934*. New York: Norton, 1934. Pp. 209–11, 265–72, 287–89.

McCarthy, Mary. *Sights and Spectacles, 1937–1956*. New York: Farrar, Straus, and Cudahy, 1956. Pp. 80–88.

Nathan, George Jean. *Passing Judgments*. New York: Knopf, 1935. Pp. 66–73, 112–26.

———. *The Theatre of the Moment*. New York: Knopf, 1936. Pp. 196–207.

———. *Theatre Book of the Year, 1946–47*. New York: Knopf, 1947. Pp. 93–111.

———. *The World of George Jean Nathan*, edited by Charles Angoff. New York: Knopf, 1952. Pp. 30–43, 395–411.

Nicoll, Allardyce. *World Drama from Æschylus to Anouilh*. New York: Harcourt, Brace, n.d. [1950?]. Pp. 880–931.

Raleigh, John H. *The Plays of Eugene O'Neill*. Carbondale: Southern Illinois University Press, 1965.

Shipley, Joseph T. *The Art of Eugene O'Neill*. University of Washington Chapbooks No. 13. Seattle: University of Washington Book Store, 1928.

Sievers, W. David. *Freud on Broadway*. New York: Hermitage House, 1955. Pp. 97–133.

Skinner, Richard Dana. *Eugene O'Neill, A Poet's Quest*. New York: Longmans, Green, 1935.

Spiller, Robert E. *The Cycle of American Literature*. New York: Macmillan, 1955. Pp. 243–74.

Winther, Sophus Keith. *Eugene O'Neill, A Critical Study*. New York: Random House, 1934.

Young, Stark. *Immortal Shadows*. New York: Scribner's, 1948. Pp. 61–66, 91–95, 132–39, 261–64.

ARTICLES

Alexander, Doris M. "*Strange Interlude* and Schopenhauer," *American Literature*, 25:213–28 (May 1953).

———. "Psychological Fate in *Mourning Becomes Electra*," *PMLA*, 68:923–34 (December 1953).

Asselnian, Roger. "*Mourning Becomes Electra* as a Tragedy," *Modern Drama*, 1:143–50 (December 1958).

Conlin, Matthew T. "The Tragic Effect in *Autumn Fire* and *Desire under the Elms*," *Modern Drama*, 1:228–35 (February 1959).

Falk, Doris V. "That Paradox, O'Neill," *Modern Drama*, 6:221–38 (December 1963).

Fergusson, Francis. "Eugene O'Neill," *Hound and Horn*, 3:145–60 (January–March 1930).

Frenz, Horst. "Eugene O'Neill's Plays Printed Abroad," *College English*, 5:340–41 (March 1944).

Herbert, Edward. "Eugene O'Neill: An Evaluation by Fellow Playwrights," *Modern Drama*, 6:239–40 (December 1963).

Isaacs, Edith J. R. "Meet Eugene O'Neill," *Theatre Arts*, 30:576–87 (October 1946).

"The Ordeal of Eugene O'Neill," *Time*, 48:71–78 (October 21, 1946).

Raleigh, John Henry. "O'Neill's Long Day's Journey into Night and New England Irish-Catholicism," *Partisan Review*, 26:573–92 (Fall 1959).

Weissman, Philip. "Conscious and Unconscious Autobiographical Dramas of Eugene O'Neill," *Journal of the American Psychoanalytic Association*, 5:432–60 (July 1957).

Weigand, Charmion von. "The Quest of Eugene O'Neill," *New Theatre*, 2:12–17, 30–32 (September 1935).